Help Them,
Heal Them,
Set Them Free

Help Them, Heal Them, Set Them Free

Rescue and Care of Injured Wild Animals

Melita Zahnke Meyer

WITH ILLUSTRATIONS BY THE AUTHOR

Tidewater Publishers, Centreville, Maryland

Library of Congress Cataloging in Publication Data

Meyer, Melita Zahnke, 1916-
        Help them, heal them, set them free.

        Summary: Describes the work of the Chesapeake Bird and Wildlife Sanctuary and how it cares for injured wild animals.
  1. Chesapeake Bird and Wildlife Sanctuary—Juvenile literature.   2. Wildlife rescue—Chesapeake Bay Region—Juvenile literature.   3. Wildlife rescue— Maryland—Prince George's County—Juvenile literature. [1. Chesapeake Bird and Wildlife Sanctuary. 2. Wildlife rescue—Chesapeake Bay Region] I. Title.
QL83.2.M48 1985   639.9'6'0975251   85-40584
ISBN 0-87033-337-2

Manufactured in the United States of America

First edition

This book is for
     my daughter, Melita Wynn Williams,
       and my granddaughter,
         Heather Melita,
because this book is about life
     and the continuation of life.

These people made this book possible:

Dianne Pearce, Margaret Dobi, and John Vincent who shared their adventures of rescuing birds, small mammals, and a deer. Dianne Pearce's devotion, dedication, and knowledge of wildlife spurred me on to write about the need for protecting our environment and the wildlife in our backyards.

Jane Ockershausen Smith for her constant encouraging comments and criticisms and members of her creative writing class who listened to and also criticized the stories.

Heather Williams, Laura Lee, and Aime Carlson and students at Fountainblue Elementary School, Hagerstown, Maryland, who listened to the stories and liked the drawings. Melita Wynn Williams who typed and proofread the entire manuscript.

Elise Meyer Baylis who made the necessary corrections on her word processor.

Flora Gaarden, Carol Toepper, and Leah Schlenker for proofreading the manuscript.

But, above all, Wiff who picks up the pieces without complaining when I fall apart.

—Pedie

Contents

1. A Bird in the Bush, 1
2. Chip, Chipper, the Robin, 3
3. The Bird Lady of the Sanctuary, 5
4. A Helper Extraordinaire, 7
5. Helpers of Every Color, 10
6. Baby Birds, Baby Birds, Baby Birds, 11
7. Ugly Birds, Unique Habits!, 14
8. The "Ole" Turkey Buzzard, 17
9. It Wouldn't Let Go!, 20
10. The Jailbird, 23
11. A Tale about a Tail, 25
12. She's a King!, 28
13. Motorcycle Owl, 30
14. Saga of the Silent Quartet!, 32
15. Saga of the Silent Quartet—Continued, 34
16. The Littlest Owl, 36
17. Feathered Horns, 38
18. Baby Talk for the General, 40
19. An Unnatural Mother, 44
20. The Proud Peacock, 46
21. The Phantom Pheasant, 48
22. Swans by Any Other Name, 50
23. High-Flying Honker, 52
24. The Squawking Goose, 54
25. Hummy, 56

26. Pigeon Heaven, 59

27. Pigeon, Pigeon, Who's Got the Pigeon?, 61

28. The Subway Pigeon, 64

29. Oh, Annabell! Oh, Annabell!, 66

30. Kelly, the Green Heron, 68

31. Long-Legged Beauties, 70

32. A Four-Legged Foster Mother, 72

33. Nestle, 75

34. Quackers and Cheese, 76

35. Disco Duck, 78

36. Cheese Did It!, 80

37. Ducks Don't Drink Beer, 82

38. Now You See Them, Now You Don't, 84

39. To the Rescue!, 87

40. Epilogue to the Rescue, 90

41. Squirrels of Every Color, 91

42. The Little Thieves or Ferrets, 94

43. The Three-Legged Fox, 96

44. A Trio of Fawns, 99

45. A Deer Not So Dear!, 103

46. The Groundhog or Woodchuck, 107

47. Cats, Cats, Cats!, 110

48. Corky, the Cockatiel, 112

49. How to Be a Bird Nurse, 114

50. A New Home for Birds and Beasts, 116

Help Them,
  Heal Them,
    Set Them Free

1. A Bird in the Bush

These stories begin
         with a bird in the bush.
The neighbor who rang our doorbell
         said there was an injured bird
                  fluttering around the shrubbery.
It was a mourning dove
         and was trying to fly
                  but couldn't keep its balance.
If we were to leave it out there,
         it would be an easy prey for a cat or dog.
We put a towel over the bird
                  so it wouldn't flap its wings frantically
                           and injure itself further.
We also thought it wise
         to cover our hands.
Its beak and claws
         might be carrying germs harmful to people.
We put it in a box
         with some birdseed.
The next morning the bird was still alive
         but hadn't touched the food.
What could we do?
         The bird would starve
                  without proper care.
Veterinarians are very expensive
         and many of them
                  will not treat wild birds.
We called the Society for the Prevention of Cruelty to Animals
         and learned about Dianne Pearce
                  and the Chesapeake Bird and Wildlife Sanctuary.

Our bird was taken to the Sanctuary
and Dianne examined it.
It had extensive brain damage
and could have flown into a window
or been hit by a car.
It lived for a few days
with food and good care.

If you find an injured bird,
call a local veterinarian,
the Society for the Prevention of Cruelty to Animals,
the local Audubon Society,
or a naturalist
at a state or national park.
One of them will know
of a licensed rehabilitator in your area
who will take care of an injured bird,
free of charge.

2. Chip, Chipper, the Robin

Dianne became a bird rehabilitator in 1980
    when she rescued Chipper, a robin.
Robins hop around on the wet ground
    early in the morning
        looking for worms.
Dogs, too, like to get up at dawn
    to sniff around in the neighborhood,
        and two of them
            thought the bobbing robin
                was a fascinating plaything.
They chased it back and forth,
    playing with it,
        and didn't know they were hurting it.
But Dianne who saw them
    yelled loudly,
        firmly,
            and with authority like a teacher.
The beagle,
    that seldom dropped anything,
        was so startled by Dianne's shout,
          he let the bird go.
Dianne scooped it up
    before the dogs
        could continue their game
          of chase and grab.
She washed it, fed it,
    and called many people for help,
        but no one seemed to care.
           Just an ordinary robin,
             they said.

Dianne finally located a bird rehabilitator,
   who took care of wild birds.
      She told Dianne how to bandage the wings
         so they would heal properly.
Dianne wasn't very hopeful that the robin would live
   but decided that while it was alive,
      she would keep it safe, warm, and fed.
To her delight a few days later,
   the robin was hopping around in the house,
      chirping merrily, perching on her shoulder,
         sleeping on her chest when she napped,
            and answering her with a chip, chip, chip.
Chipper's story
   was told and retold in the neighborhood,
      and people began bringing other birds to Dianne.
Dianne read books,
   took courses with veterinarians
      and bird rehabilitators,
         and asked question after question
            of doctors, nurses,
               and ornithologists who study birds.
She met all the requirements
   of the state and federal governments
      to keep all kinds of birds except eagles.
And that's how
   the Chesapeake Bird and Wildlife Sanctuary
      was hatched!

3. The Bird Lady of the Sanctuary

No bird is turned away
     from the Chesapeake Bird and Wildlife Sanctuary.
No matter how sick,
     how battered,
        or how ugly,
           any bird is welcomed.
Dianne Pearce, the bird lady,
     who started the Sanctuary in her home,
        was a fashion model
           at the age of twelve.
For many years
     her feet were seen in newspaper ads

in elegant heels,
        sturdy Hush Puppies,
                or white tennis sneakers.

Now her feet are bare,
      most of the time,
          and she runs from patio to garage,
              up and down stairs,
                  tending with her hands
                      battered and injured wildlife.

She has a degree in psychology
      and ran a successful talent agency from her home.
Day and night she nurses sick and dying birds,
      and cares for rabbits, squirrels, raccoons,
          six pet cats, two dogs, and a pair of cockatiels.
She takes them to veterinarians
      and pediatricians
        for X rays, operations, and injections.
She feeds the birds
      dead mice, fish heads, worms, birdseed,
        and decaying vegetables
          that she begs or buys
            from stores and restaurants.
When the birds are too sick to eat,
      she force-feeds them through a tube.
She bandages and bathes them,
      exercises them,
        and gently strokes them
          with her healing hands.
Every creature with a spark of life is cared for
      day and night because Dianne and her helpers
        have a deep respect for all living things,
          including the birds that many people consider trash
            such as pigeons and starlings!
"My happiest moment," she says,
      "is when I see the tail of a bird
        disappearing over the trees."

4. A Helper Extraordinaire

Margaret, Dianne's mother and special helper,
    gripped the wheel of the car.
Her eyes darted from the road
    to the speedometer.
This was not the time
    to be stopped
        by a policeman for speeding.
Out of the corner of her eye
    she watched her daughter,
        who was holding a pigeon in her hands
            and shaking it periodically
                to restore its breathing.
When it lapsed into a coma,
    Dianne would jolt it again.
The veterinarian's office
    was crowded with people and pets.
The men and women stared,
    the cats snarled,
        and the dogs growled
            as Dianne continued to shake the pigeon
                back to life.
The receptionist frowned
    and went into the office
        to talk to the doctor.
When she came back,
    she shook her head.
        The vet would not treat the bird.
Dianne and her mother got back into the car.
    They drove onto the Beltway
        over the Potomac River to Virginia
        to another veterinarian
            thirty miles away.

Margaret's eyes
    shifted back and forth
        to the road, to the speedometer, and to the rearview mirror.
She gasped
        when she saw Dianne put her mouth
            to the beak of the unconscious pigeon.
Dianne was giving the pigeon
        mouth-to-mouth resuscitation
            and continued to do so until they came
                to the vet's office
The vet examined the pigeon
        and shook his head sadly.
            The injuries were so extensive
                that the pigeon could not breathe by itself.

Margaret has spent many hours on winding roads
        in snow and rain and sleet,
            and drove 150 miles in one day
                to rescue a bird.
One weekend she flew over a thousand miles
        to pick up a bird.
One of Dianne's friends
        had a crow
            that needed a foster home
                and begged Dianne to take it.
Margaret's son, who is an airline pilot,
        was able to get her a free pass
            on his airline,
                and she flew
                    to Connecticut to pick up the crow.
Margaret is also a licensed caretaker
        and bandages and medicates birds.

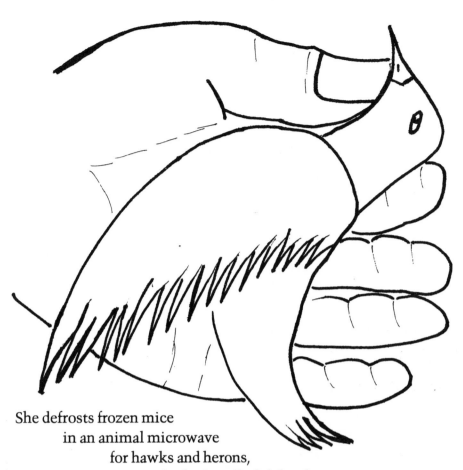

She defrosts frozen mice
     in an animal microwave
         for hawks and herons,
            she feeds gulls fish heads,
              and with an eyedropper
                  she gives baby birds their formulas.
She cleans the garage, patio, and bathroom
     where a green heron was allowed to fly freely.
She runs a shop
     that sells antiques and crafts
         to raise money for the Sanctuary.
She answers the telephone,
     takes messages,
         and contacts Dianne on her beeper
            for emergency instructions.
But most of all,
     she is there
         to lend a hand
            when Dianne is saving a life.

5. Helpers of Every Color

Like birds,
    volunteers come in every size, shape, age,
        and colored fur, or rather hair.
Four of the Sanctuary's most faithful and dedicated helpers
    are Vicky, a redhead,
        Yvonne, a brunette, and
            Nichole and Stephanie, blonds.
Their fathers are policemen,
    and they are all under fourteen years of age.
No task has been too difficult
    or too dirty for them to do,
        including scrubbing the floors
            and cleaning up the cages.
They help feed the baby birds,
    bottle-feed the squirrels,
        and beg to fix Dianne's dinner.
They answer the telephone,
    call people about their birds,
        and urge people to come to meetings.
If callers are greeted by giggles,
    not songs,
        they are talking
            to one of these willing helpers.
These four volunteers also give tours of the Sanctuary to visitors,
    and they can recite the history of all the birds and mammals
        without a script.
At the Oktoberfest
    they took turns dancing about
        in a Woodsey the Owl costume
            as they sold donated items,
                popcorn, and hot dogs.

6. Baby Birds, Baby Birds, Baby Birds

In the springtime,
  the telephone at the Sanctuary
    rings and rings
      every few minutes,
        day and late into the night.
People bring baby robins,
  starlings, crows, bluebirds, swallows,
    and one time a yellow-billed cuckoo.
There have been as many as
  fifty birds in the nursery
    at the same time.
Once a lady brought three eggs
  she had found on the ground.
    Dianne put them into an incubator,
      and hoped they would hatch.
Lo and behold, three naked babies
  emerged from the eggs the next day.
When their feathers grew in,
  Dianne knew that they were robins.

Nests with baby birds
  are blown out of trees by windstorms.
Some babies fall to the ground
  when they lean out too far
    reaching for food.

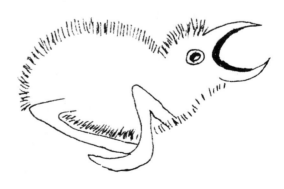

Sometimes trees
      are cut down, and the frightened mothers
         fly away.
If you find babies on the ground,
      it is best to put them
         back into their nest.
The parents will feed them
      even if they have been touched by people.

Baby birds learn to beg for food
      and will peep as soon as Dianne or a helper
         comes into the nursery.

But birds know that the cats aren't friends,
    and they don't make a sound
        when a cat sneaks into the nursery.
When the birds are very young,
    they must be fed a special formula
        from an eyedropper every half an hour.
Feeding dozens of birds
    keeps Dianne and her helpers
        running up and down the stairs
           all day long.
Fortunately, for bird parents
    and Sanctuary helpers,
        baby birds sleep
           during the dark or nighttime hours.

Mammals, such as baby squirrels, rabbits, and human babies
    have to be fed day and night
        around the clock.
Baby bird mouths are lined with bright colors,
    pink, red, purple, or yellow.
        Baby barn swallows have a white streak
           like a mustache above their mouths.
Nature colors their mouths
    so the parent birds
        can find the right place
           to drop the food.

When the birds grow up,
    Dianne puts them out on the patio.
They learn to pick up their own food
    and practice flying
        from the fence to the cages.
One day they take off,
    happy to be on their own,
        but a lazy starling
           comes back daily for a free meal.

7. Ugly Birds, Unique Habits!

The wildlife worker
  was fishing at Mayo Beach
    when he spotted the vulture
      that many people call a "buzzard,"
        floating in the water.
It was trapped in a web of fish lines and weeds.
  If left there, the vulture would drown.
Putting on his gloves
  to protect his hands,
    the wildlife worker pulled the bird into his boat.
A frightened, injured buzzard
  might scratch with its claws
    or bite with its beak.
Just barely alive, he thought,
  when he felt a faint heartbeat.
He cut away the fish lines and entangling weeds
  from the soaked feathers.
Hoping it would recover in the sun,
  he put the vulture on the pier
    to rest and dry out,
      and then he went fishing.
When he returned many hours later,
  he hoped he wouldn't find a dead bird,
    and was happy to see
      that the vulture was moving.
He placed it into a bushel basket,
  put a cover over it,
    and brought it to the Sanctuary.
Its head hung low, and it was so tired
  that it didn't spit at Dianne
    when she examined it.

She put it into a large cage
        with some other recuperating birds
                where it could continue to rest
                        and to practice flying later.
The other birds avoided it,
        but another vulture joined it at its feast
                of dead mice or "carrion."
This buzzard, already in the cage, had been found
        in an illegal trap in a field in Upper Marlboro.
One of its legs was badly infected
        because it had been left in the trap so long.
Dianne rushed the bird
        to a veterinarian
                and shed a few tears
                        when he had to amputate the infected leg.
Some people consider vultures ugly
        with their naked, red fleshy heads,
                but Dianne and other rehabilitators
                        know that these birds
                                have a very important place
                                        in the balance of nature.
Therefore, they protect and care for them
        as they would a swan
                or a bird with beautiful feathers.
Vultures are extraordinary creatures.
        Unlike hawks, eagles, and owls,
                they do not catch live animals.
                        They eat dead ones.
Vultures have been seen
        refusing to eat from a pile of supposedly dead chickens
                because one of the chickens showed signs of life.
They can eat decaying meat or carrion
        because their stomachs
                contain powerful bacteria
                        that destroy germs
                                which could pollute our land and water
                                        and kill our plants and animals.

Vultures clean up an environment
        that thoughtless people and animals
                litter with trash and garbage.
In some small villages in South America,
        vultures are the only means of sanitation.
Vultures stick their bare heads
        into any mess, even cavities or "holes" in dead animals.
                Since they have no feathers on their heads,
                        they don't scatter germs
                                as they fly from carcass to carcass.
A turkey buzzard flies close to the ground
        and when it smells decaying matter
                will dive for it.
Suddenly a flock will appear in the empty sky
        to share the feast.
When vultures are threatened
        by other predators or people,
                they will spit, throw up, or play dead.

Dianne had to prepare a special diet for the two vultures.
        A month later the one-legged bird was hopping around in his cage.
A raptor specialist, who takes care of birds of prey, examined both birds,
        and said they were well enough to fly free.
                They took off without a backward glance
                        at their human, live nurse.

8. The "Ole" Turkey Buzzard

"There's a big bird hanging from a tree,"
    said the lady on the telephone.
Dianne asked her many questions,
    but the more she heard
        the more puzzled she became.
She and her friend, John Vincent, a Sanctuary volunteer,
    drove to a nearby town
        and had no difficulty finding the hanging bird.
They followed the parade of people and cars,
    a long hook and ladder truck,
        and an ambulance
            that had responded
                to someone's frantic call.
"It's a turkey vulture," said Dianne
    when she saw the predator
        dangling from the tall oak.
Strands of fish line were wrapped around one wing
    and the string had become entangled
        in the branches of a tree.
            The tree was taller than a telephone pole.
How the bird got caught in the fish line
    and then flew to the tree
        will always remain the bird's secret!
The helpless vulture swung in the wind,
    spitting at the crowd below,
        its claws clutching at the empty air.
Dianne talked to the reluctant firemen
    and told them that spitting was the usual behavior
        for a vulture when frightened.
"Fortunately, he hasn't eaten recently
    or he might throw up," she said.

The firemen shook their heads.
They weren't about to go up
and rescue that angry creature.
It wasn't their kind of a problem.
Someone called the Baltimore Gas and Electric Company,
and as they waited and watched the bird,
Dianne hoped the wing wasn't broken
and permanently damaged
by its frantic struggling.
When the repairman from the Gas Company
got out of his truck,
he snorted, "Just an 'ole' turkey buzzard."
And he, too, shook his head.
No way was he about to touch that snarling animal.
But he said that John could use the cherry picker
to rescue the bird.
He showed John how to use the controls of the machine.
With a long-handled pruner,
or three-foot scissors,
to cut away the branches and fish lines,
John took off.
He maneuvered the basket of the cherry picker
going up and sideways at the same time
and then it stopped—
three feet away from the buzzard.
It couldn't go any higher.
Using the pruner to reach the bird,
John managed to loop some cord
around the grasping claws
and tie them together.
After a few more jerky starts and stops,
John moved the basket directly under the vulture.
He carefully cut away the lines and branches,
and the bird fell into the cherry picker.
John bent down
out of sight of the onlookers
to tend to the buzzard.

Suddenly a howl of pain
      burst out of the basket.
The ungrateful bird
    had bitten
        the hand that had rescued it!

9. It Wouldn't Let Go!

The family of four
        were taking an outing
                in their boat on the Patuxent River.
"Look," said one of the kids.
        "There's a big brown bird
                floating in the water."
They circled the bird
        a number of times.
It wasn't moving.
        The father thought it could be a hawk
                because of its size and brown feathers tipped with white.
They rode on, but the children
        kept looking back.
Suddenly one of the kids shouted,
        "Look, it's trying to raise its head."
They went back to the bird.
        It was struggling
                and gasping for air.
The father covered his hands with plastic bags
        to protect them before he lifted the bird out of the water.
Its feathers were water soaked
        and that's why it couldn't fly.
With a few more minutes in the water
        it would sink and drown.
They took the hawk
        to the game warden.
He said it was an osprey fledgling
        or "fish hawk" just learning to fly.

It may have flown too far away from its nest
        and couldn't fly back.
Or it could have caught a fish
        too big to carry
                and had been dragged into the water.
Ospreys hover above the water
        watching for fish to swim to the surface.
They plunge down, feet first,
        and grasp the fish with their spiked talons.
                The weight of the fish
                        causes their claws to lock onto it
                                so it won't be dropped as the bird flies.
Ospreys also have scales on the bottom of their feet
        to hold the slippery fish.

The game warden brought the osprey
        to the Sanctuary to rest after its unexpected swim.
It had a U. S. band on its leg.
        Since ospreys are a threatened species,
                conservationists study them
                        to find out where they fly and what they eat.
Dianne called Steve Cardona,
        who bands birds in her area,
                and read the serial number to him.
He checked his notes,
        and sure enough it was one of his birds.
                He knew where the bird's nest was located.
He invited Dianne to accompany him
        on his catamaran or sailboat
                two miles down the river
                        to take the osprey to its nest.
When they came within sight of it,
        an untidy pile of sticks
                perched on a platform on a pole
                        out in the water,
                                he released the bird.
The bird flew away over the treetops,
        not to its nest.
"Very good," said Steve.
        "It's old enough to be on its own."
It will find a mate
        and build its own nest
                on a pole, dead tree, or a platform out in the water.
Maybe it has learned
        to catch small fish,
                not fish too big to carry!

10. The Jailbird

The prisoners at the D.C. Jail
       whose cells overlooked the exercise yard
            saw the bird lying on the ground.
It was about the size of a robin
       with black stripes on its rusty red back and tail.
The bird would flutter around on the ground,
       vainly trying to fly,
            but then would lapse into a coma
               or become unconscious.
One of the guards
       picked it up.
"Let it go," shouted the prisoners.
       "Let it fly away."
"Sure thing," said the guard,
       "when it's okay.
           I'm taking it to someone who can care for it."
He put it into a large paper bag
       and brought it to the Sanctuary.
"It's a kestrel," said Dianne,
       "sometimes called a sparrow hawk or falcon."

She examined it
>and couldn't find any broken bones.
It was conscious now
>but when it tried to fly
>>it would fall back to the ground.
"It bumped into something," said Dianne.
>"Fortunately, it isn't a peregrine falcon.
>>They dive at speeds up to 175 miles an hour!
>>When they hit something,
>>>they rarely survive.
The kestrel dives
>at its prey, but it prefers
>>to hover like a helicopter
>>>as it feeds on insects."
Dianne put this hawk into a cage
>with a female kestrel.
In a few days he was eating,
>and the pair seemed happy together.
When Dianne opened the cage,
>off they flew,
>>the female leading the way.
Dianne called the guard at the D.C. Jail
>to let the inmates know
>>that their bird had gone over the fence
>>>to freedom.

11. A Tale about a Tail

The hawk stared into space
    with its large, yellow, unblinking eyes
        and didn't look dizzy or disoriented.
It had been hit by a car
    and had a head injury.
        Also, all of its tail feathers
            had been pulled out
                during the accident.
It recovered from the concussion
    in a few days,
        but the loss of its tail feathers
            might cause it difficulty.

Hawks have large wings
    to fly and soar or float
        on the warm air drafts
            that rise from the earth.
But their tails
    are their rudders
        that help them keep their balance,
            to fly straight,
                and to turn right and left.

This hawk could fly
    but without its tail
        it might go hungry in the coming winter.
Hawks catch live prey
    such as rats and snakes
        and should capture them on their first approach.

If the hawk's aim isn't accurate the first time,
　　　　its meal could scamper or slither away.
Dianne dismissed the thought
　　　　　　of cooping it up in a cage for months
　　　　　　　　until its tail feathers grew in.
It would be too unhappy
　　　　and could lose some of its hunting skills.
She called her friend, Michael Moreland.
　　　　　　Michael's father, a falcon trainer,
　　　　　　　　had taught him how to replace or "impinge"
　　　　　　　　　　feathers in birds.
He came to the Sanctuary
　　　　with his bag of feathers
　　　　　　that he gathers from dead birds.
Feathers grow out of shafts or tubes.
　　　　　　Every spring old ones drop off,
　　　　　　　　and new ones come out.
While Dianne held the bird
　　　　firmly by its legs,
　　　　　　Michael cut some bobby pins to size.
He stuck them into the shafts with super glue.
　　　　　　He put more glue on the other end of the pins
　　　　　　　　and stuck a feather on each one
　　　　　　　　　　carefully graduating them
　　　　　　　　　　　　in a semicircle.
They talked to the bird quietly
　　　　as they worked,
　　　　　　and the hawk didn't try to peck them.
　　　　　　　　It seemed to sense they were trying to help.
They placed the hawk back into a cage
　　　　to allow the glue to dry.
After forty-five minutes
　　　　they decided it was time to let it go.

26

Would the tail work?
>When they opened the door,
>>the bird hopped to the doorway,
>>>looked about,
>>>>and, without hesitation
>>>>>or a backward glance
>>>>>>at its doctors,
>>>>>>>took off.

It soared high above the trees,
>gliding right and left,
>>flying as gracefully
>>>as though it had never
>>>>lost its tail.

But this fall
>there might be some puzzled bird-watchers
>>in southern Maryland.
A new species of hawk
>could be reported
>>because Michael
>>>had impinged red-tailed feathers
>>>>into a red-shouldered hawk!

12. She's a King!

Mariah, the stately golden eagle,
    looked about her proudly
        from her high perch in her flight cage.
This was the behavior
    that one would expect
        from the king of birds.
Many nations—
    the Roman Empire, Prussia, Russia,
        France under Napoleon, and the United States—
            have adopted the eagle
                as their symbol
because this majestic bird
    is famous for its
        strength and courage.
There are two types of eagles in the United States,
    the bald, our national bird,
        and the golden, both endangered species.
Eagles have the remarkable ability to soar
    on drafts of warm air that rise from the earth,
        but Mariah will never join her sisters in the sky.
Feathers on one wing were damaged in the wild
    and can't be repaired.
She was found in Minnesota
    and flown by airplane
        to a Maryland breeding and rehabilitation center
            for endangered species.
The center is raising bald eagles
    and has so many
        they no longer had a cage for Mariah.
When the naturalist called the Sanctuary,
    Dianne was delighted to give the eagle a home
        but had to get special permission
            from the Government
                to keep her.

Golden eagles are on the endangered list
　　　　because many years ago thousands of them
　　　　　　were slaughtered by ranchers in the West.
The ranchers thought these predators
　　　　were carrying off their lambs and calves.
　　　　　　Recent studies have found, however,
　　　　　　　　that eagles eat mostly prairie dogs and mice.
When Mariah is full-grown,
　　　　she will weigh about thirteen pounds,
　　　　　　·　slightly more than a male.
Therefore, it is very unlikely
　　　　that farm animals that weigh more than eagles
　　　　　　would have been snatched by these birds of prey.
Dianne must wear heavy gloves
　　　　that cover her lower arms completely
　　　　　　when she examines Mariah
　　　　　　　　because the eagle's claws are so strong
　　　　　　　　　　they could crush Dianne's bones.
Like the king of birds, that she is,
　　　　Mariah holds her head proudly aloft
　　　　　　to display her golden-tipped feathers
　　　　　　　　at the nape of her neck
　　　　　　　　　　when she is admired by visitors.

13. Motorcycle Owl

Dianne heard the motorcycles
    long before they stopped
        in front of the Sanctuary.
            It was two o'clock in the morning.
She peeked out of the window.
    Dressed in leather jackets,
        their faces hidden by helmets and masks,
            the men looked like creatures from outer space
              or characters in a horror movie.
Except for the birds and cats,
    Dianne was alone in the house
        and had hoped they'd pass by.
The doorbell rang once, twice,
    and then with a steady buzz.
She went to answer the doorbell
    before they awakened the neighbors.
        She didn't want any complaints
        about her Sanctuary.

Opening the door a crack,
    she could see one of the men
        holding a barred owl.
"Lady, we've got a bird here.
    One of us hit it.
        It's still alive."
"Lady," said another one, "we didn't mean to frighten you,
    but we couldn't leave this bird in the road.
        Some fellow in the gas station
            said you take care of sick birds."
Dianne opened the door
    and they all crowded into the hall.
They watched anxiously
    as she examined the bird.
"No broken bones,"
    she assured them.
        "But it is disoriented, dizzy,
            and needs a few days of rest."
The young men apologized for disturbing her
    at that hour of the night
        and wheeled their bikes
            quietly down the block
                to the main highway.
The owl was put into a cage
    to recuperate from its jarring experience.
It recovered in a few days
    and flew away
        to catch more mice and rats,
            some of human society's worst enemies.

14. Saga of the Silent Quartet!

If the four barred owls
          were children,
                    we would call them rude.
Perched on a pole
          in their large flight cage,
                    three of them stared at us
                              with their ping-pong-sized black eyes.
Merlin, the fourth one,
          seemed to wink at us
                    because one of his eyes
                              was only a slit.
                                        He had been injured by a car.
Their chests were beautifully
          streaked with bars
                    of gray, brown, and white feathers.
Their bright yellow noses
          looked like witches' beaks.
Dianne put on her heavy gloves
          and grasped Merlin by his legs,
                    stroking him gently to calm him.
"Merlin's eye may get better," she said,
          "but the other three have damaged wings
                    and only time will tell
                              whether they will fly again."
If not, they would be kept at the Sanctuary
          for students to study them.
They might be mated,
          and the babies raised at the Sanctuary
                    would be released to fly free.
Merlin's eye healed,
          and he was taken back to Greenbelt Park
                    where he was found.

Owls usually mate for life
and Merlin may have had a wife and babies
waiting for him.
But before he was released
Don Patterson, a photographer,
took his picture.
This picture was on the cover
of the Upper Marlboro Telephone Directory
and his story was on the inside.
Many people have read
about Merlin
and hopefully will drive more carefully
to avoid injuring
the young and old of all species.

After Merlin was released
 one of the other owls,
  a young one,
   recovered its ability to fly
    and was also released.
But sad to tell,
 the ability to fly
  is not the only reason
   for releasing a bird of prey.
A few days after it flew away,
 a neighbor called
  and asked Dianne
   if she had released an owl recently.
She said she had seen
 the owl hovering around her mailbox.
Owls are rarely seen in the daytime.
 That's why she knew it was in trouble.
She had no difficulty
 capturing it
  because it was so weak.

Dianne picked it up
        and realized that she had released it too soon.
Although owls have a natural instinct
        to chase and catch live prey,
                they must have time to practice their skills
                        in order to survive in the wild.
Later Dianne visited a refuge near Chicago
        where owls are raised,
                and handicapped ones are rehabilitated.
She saw a type of large flight cage
        where live rats and mice can run about and not get out.
Young hawks and owls can practice
        catching live prey in them
                before they are released.
She has the plans for this kind of cage,
        and two members of the Sanctuary
                have volunteered to build it.
The threesome is a quartet again.
        A baby barred owl
                that had been blown out of its nest
                        was brought to the Sanctuary.
But this owl and all other owls
        will not be released
                until Dianne is sure they can catch their own meals!

16. The Littlest Owl

The screech owl was crouched
    in the back of the cage.
It was about the size of a robin
    but plumper with a short broad tail.
It can look much larger
    when it fluffs up its feathers
        to keep warm.
The tufts of feathers on its head,
    which look like ears but aren't,
        seemed to perk up at the sound
            of Dianne's voice.
It turned its head,
    swivelling it around completely,
        until it looked as if it were on backwards.
Since owls cannot roll their eyes
    like human beings,
        they must turn their heads
            to see to the sides.
This owl had been shot in the left eye
    by a hunter or a careless child with a BB gun.
The veterinarian said he couldn't restore
    its sight.
It will not be released
    because it will not be able to hunt very well.
Also, since it is blind on one side,
    it would not be able to see its enemies
        if they attacked from that side.
Screech owls do not screech or scream.
    Their call is like a wail
        that gets lower and lower.
Dianne will weigh it
    to find out what sex it is.
        If it is a female, it will weigh more than a male.

Some day she may find a mate for it.
　　If babies are raised at the Sanctuary,
　　　　they would be released into the wild
　　　　　　but not until they can catch their own food
　　　　　　　and protect themselves.

17. Feathered Horns

The great horned owl
    kept its face in the corner
       like a sulking child
         who had been punished.
"It's disoriented," said Dianne.
    "It was hit by an unknown object,
       probably a car."
Putting on her heavy gloves
    to keep the claws from scratching her,
       she grasped it firmly by its legs
         and turned it around.
One eye was closed
    but it stared at her
       with its good, huge, yellow-rimmed one.
       Suddenly it blinked.

"Owls are the only birds
           that can wink,
                   but they pull up their lower lids
                           when they sleep during the daytime
                               just like other birds."
Dianne parted the feathers
           on one side of the owl's head,
                   exposing a perfectly formed ear.
"The owl's horns look like ears
           but are only tufts of feathers."
She spread out one of its wings,
           and it stretched out nearly as long as her arm.
There are many different kinds of owls in the world
           but the great horned owl is one of the largest.
When Dianne put the owl back into its cage,
                   it retreated to the rear again
                           turning its checkered gray, brown, and white
                               feathered back to her.

A few weeks later
           the eye remained open,
                   and the owl no longer turned its back
                           to the visitors who came to admire it.
A raptor specialist,
           who works with birds of prey,
                   examined it
                           and said it had recovered its sight
                               and could be released.
"Don't let your pet out at night," said Dianne,
           "if there's a great horned owl around.
                   They hunt at night and sleep during the day.
                       They have the most remarkable eyesight and hearing
                               and can catch a mouse in complete darkness.
                                   Cats have been known to disappear
                                       without a sound."

18. Baby Talk for the General

"The General" is a crow,
a sassy, inquisitive bird
that speaks one word—"caw"—over and over again.
But in that one word the crow can express
curiosity, fear, fury, or glee.
The General will also click his beak
when he wants attention.
He had been a pet
and was kept in a cage in an apartment.
The man of the house wanted to release him
but the man's wife said that The General must be rehabilitated
before they let him go.
He had not learned to fear his natural enemies
and would open his mouth
begging for junk food
from people, cats, and dogs.
The wife brought him to the Sanctuary,
and before Dianne could put him into a cage,
he flew over the fence
toward the woods.
Dianne grabbed a fresh piece of meat
from the refrigerator,
and she and her mother, Margaret,
scurried to their car
in pursuit of the bird.
If he took off into the woods,
they would never find him.
Fortunately, he landed on a TV antenna
two blocks away.
Dianne waved the meat
trying to lure him down
as she talked to him softly.

No response!
>The General looked toward the woods
>>and spread his wings.
Dianne continued to cajole and coax.
>Children gathered, shouting, and laughing,
>>at the strange scene.
Margaret spread her arms wide
>to keep them away from Dianne,
>>pleading with them to be quiet.
A thought kept nagging at Dianne
>as The General ignored her.
Talking, something about talking—
>she let the voice of the bird's former mistress
>>play back in her mind.
Baby talk!
>The woman had spoken baby talk to The General.
"Here, itsy-bitsy Baby, come to Mama.
>Come and get your din-din.
>>Come, Baby!"
Dianne imitated the woman's voice and tone.
>The General cocked his head.
>>Aha, thought Dianne, he hears me.

She went on and on
          feeling as silly as a parrot.
The crowd grew larger.
          Mothers carrying babies
                    and fathers with wrenches and hammers in their hands
                         gathered around.
Margaret urged them to be still
          as she marched in front of them like a sentry.
The bird on the high perch
          watched the people parade below him.
Then he hopped
          to the roof of the house.
"Come, itsy-bitsy Baby!
          Come to Mama!"
The General hopped
          to the edge of the roof.
Dianne kept her voice under control.
          The bird flew to the garage roof.
                    Over and over Dianne repeated the same silly words
                         because she couldn't think of any new ones.
The General flew to the ground.
          Cautiously, he hopped to Dianne
                    and pecked at the meat.
The crowd watched without a sound.
          With a slow, careful movement,
                    Dianne picked him up.
The crowd followed Dianne and The General
          back to the Sanctuary
                    where she clipped his wing and tail feathers.
These feathers are like hair on human beings
          and can be cut without pain
                    because they do not have nerve endings.
In the spring The General will get new feathers
          when he molts.
The General may have to become a permanent resident at the Sanctuary
          if he can't stop begging from strange creatures,
                    such as dogs and cats.

But he'll have plenty of company at the Sanctuary.
In a large flight cage, there are a dozen crows
that have broken wings
or have been pets and can't be retrained
to live in the wild.
His noisiest rival will be Kola with his broken wing,
who is constantly pecking at his dish,
demanding more mealworms.
Kola has appointed himself sergeant major
of all the birds on the patio.
He screams and complains
when someone talks to The General,
and The General caws jealously
when Kola is perched on Dianne's shoulder
ruffling her hair or tweaking her earlobes.

When Kola is on the patio,
the other birds give him plenty of room
and even the cats only watch him—
from the other side of the glass doors.

19. An Unnatural Mother

The cowbird
      with its brown head and black body
            chirped loudly
                  as it hopped about on its one good leg.
Because of an infection
      that could have killed her,
            one of her legs had been amputated.
"You're a strange one,"
      said Dianne to her.
            "But we like you anyway."
The bird cocked her head
      as though she were listening to Dianne.
Some cowbirds prefer
      foster care for their children,
            Dianne explained,
                  rather than taking care of their own babies.
These mothers lay one speckled egg
      in the nest of another species.
The mother cleverly chooses a nest
      with eggs that look like hers.
It might be the nest of a warbler,
      a vireo, or a sparrow.
Then the foster mother sits
      on the cowbird's egg along with her own eggs
            until it is hatched.
She feeds the uninvited guest
      because it is a noisy
            and demanding baby.
With their selfish habits,
      some of these intruders have been known
            to shove their foster mother's natural babies
            out of the nest.

If the foster mother knows she has a stranger in her midst,
she doesn't abandon it,
as its natural mother has.
She feeds it with her own.
The one-legged cowbird was released
after her second molt,
and in the spring
she may find another bird's nest
to lay her egg.

20. The Proud Peacock

Everyone loves them,
    everyone wants one,
        and everyone seems to have one,
            thought Dianne,
                when she received another call
                    about a straying peacock.
Peacocks are the most beautiful birds
    in the world
        with their long fantails or train
            of shimmering blue feathers
                studded with golden eyes.
The male displays his tail to the female,
    or peahen,
        during courting
            but he will also
                spread it at any time
                    it *pleases* him.
Beautiful he may be,
    but he does do his own thing!
He has a reputation for being nasty
    and can't be put with other fowl.
He also has the habit
    of straying away from home
        and wandering about in the neighborhood.
That's why the Sanctuary
    receives countless calls
        to pick up roaming peacocks.
Dianne advertises for the owners,
    but if they don't appear,
        she has many volunteers
            who will give the birds a home.

One had a string
      tied to his leg,
            and Dianne was glad
                  when the owners didn't show up.
She gave him to a neighbor
      who wouldn't treat him like a dog.
The peacock at the Sanctuary now
      wandered into a basement
            and was discovered by the lady of the house
                  standing on the sink,
                        looking out of the window.

Dianne watched the peacock
      as he paced about on the small patio
            dragging his gorgeous tail behind him.
There wasn't room for him to display it
      without invading the space
            of the ducks, geese, pigeons, swans, and rabbits.
We need a new home
      with more land,
            Dianne thought,
                  where a peacock can strut his stuff
                        without being stepped on.

21. The Phantom Pheasant

The hunter had driven
      thousands of miles
            across the country.
He had fifty pheasants
      in the back of his camper
            that he had shot in South Dakota.
When he opened the door,
      he was surprised
            to see among the dead birds
                one very alive pheasant
                    looking up at him.
"Well, well, how did you come alive?"
      he asked as he carried the bird
            from the camper.
                "You deserve a second chance!"

He brought the pheasant
    to the Sanctuary.
Dianne examined the bird
    and could find no injuries.
He had only been stunned
    by the gunshot.
Pheasants are very popular game birds
    and hunted in many parts
        of the country.
They had been hunted so widely
    that they were on the verge of extinction.
Now, there are laws
    about when and how many you can shoot.
The males are unusually beautiful
    with their long, streaming cross-barred tails,
        copper-colored breasts,
            purple greenish necks,
                ear tufts,
                    and white necklaces.
Dianne wanted to take him
    back to South Dakota
        but couldn't find anyone
            who was driving or flying there.
She decided she must find
    a place in Maryland
        where he could join a flock.
Her mother and father
    offered to take him
        to the top of Sugarloaf Mountain,
            near Frederick, Maryland.
They saw many flocks
    and when they let him go
        he joined a group
            as though he belonged there,
                not thousands of miles away!

22. Swans by Any Other Name

Whistling swans are beautiful,
    swimming or flying!
But two of them were found sitting sadly
    on the ice of a pond in a marsh
        on the Eastern Shore of Maryland.
The extreme cold weather
    had frozen many of the ponds and bogs,
        and they couldn't pull up the wild celery they eat.
Weak from hunger,
    they weren't able to continue
        their migration to warmer waters.
They were brought to the Sanctuary,
    and Dianne examined them.
There were no injuries,
    but they were starving.
Sometime later an immature swan was brought to the Sanctuary.
    Dianne knew it was a young bird
        because it was gray, not white like adult swans.
It had been shot,
    and the vet put a pin in its wing.
        He hoped it would heal properly
            but only time would tell
                whether the swan would fly again.

Dianne was worried
    that more of these beautiful birds
        might meet the fate of this adolescent.

Cranberry farmers in New Jersey
    claim that swans are damaging their crops
        and want the U. S. Government to give them
        permission to shoot them.

The swans pull up a weed
       that grows in the same bog or swamp
           as the cranberry plants.
Of course, the sensible thing to do
       would be to get rid of the weed not the swans.

Dianne took care of the three birds all winter.
       Swans live in flocks,
           and in the spring these birds
                were taken back to the Eastern Shore
                    to join a migrating band.
But don't expect to hear swans whistle
       when they fly over your house.
           They honk like Canada geese,
                and that's why conservationists
                    are trying to change their name
                        from "whistling"
                            to "tundra" swan.
These swans hatch and raise their babies
       on the plains or tundra in northern Canada.
After a summer of feeding on the lush vegetation of the tundra,
       they migrate thousands of miles
           to the southeastern states
           with their babies
               that are now nearly full-grown.

23. High-Flying Honker

One wing of the Canada goose
     dragged on the ground,
         so badly damaged by a gun shot,
             that the veterinarian couldn't repair it.
With its tall black neck
     and white chin strap,
         the goose still walked regally about on the patio
             among the noisy, scrappy ducks, geese, and seagulls.

Canada geese migrate thousands of miles in the fall
     from the icy slopes
         around the Hudson Bay in Canada
           to the marshlands
              of Delaware, Maryland, and Virginia.
In the spring they fly back to Canada
     where they lay their eggs
         and raise their babies.
They can fly as fast as a car can travel,
     forty or fifty miles an hour.
Even the babies that are born in the spring
     migrate with their flocks,
         flying in an uneven V formation.
Lying in bed at night,
     you may hear their honking
         because they migrate day and night.

But this wounded goose will never fly north.
Dianne took him to the Merkle Wildlife Refuge
in Upper Marlboro.
About sixty wild geese
stay on the Refuge all year.
Since geese mate for life,
the partners of wounded geese
remain with them
during the spring migration.
The geese that are born and raised on the Refuge
will in turn raise their babies here.
Dianne's goose will find a mate
and raise goslings in Maryland.
The second year these goslings will find mates
and, if their mates were born on the Artic tundra,
they will migrate to Canada.

24. The Squawking Goose

When it was small, the baby goose
    was a cute and cuddly ball of yellow fuzz.
It was an Easter present to a lady
    who lived in an apartment house.
But as the months went by
    the goose lost its baby feathers
      and became an awkward, clumsy teenager.
This apartment house, like most,
    had the rule
      that pets weren't allowed to share rooms.
When the goose only peeped,
    no one could hear it
      but when it was bigger and began to squawk,
        the neighbors were disturbed by its calls
          and complained to the manager.

Geese are not trainable, like dogs,
      and this one never knew
           when to keep its mouth shut.
It squawked at night, during the day,
      when someone came to visit,
           and when it was alone.
In fact, it squawked all the time.
      Friends suggested they have a goose dinner,
           but the lady said, "No, no, no!"
She brought the goose to the Sanctuary,
      and Dianne put it out on the patio
           with the ducks, geese, and seagulls.
Here, too, it squawked and squawked
      as it snatched food from shy birds.
The neighbors would be complaining
      about the noise soon!
           Besides it ate too much,
              thought Dianne.
The goose needed a new home!
      Dianne lured it into a large cage
           and took it to the Oxon Hill Children's Farm.
There the goose lives very happily
      with other geese and ducks
           squawking at the horses
              that share the barnyard.
Bus loads of children come to the Farm
      to admire it
           and no one cares how much or how loudly
              it squawks!

25. Hummy

A mother of two children
      brought the little green hummingbird
        to the Sanctuary.
"It was fluttering around in the yard.
      We think it has a broken wing."
She watched anxiously
      as Dianne moved her hand gently over the creature
        that was only as long as her little finger.
"I can't feel any broken bones.
      It may be sprained and will heal," she said.
"The children called it 'Hummy.'
      They didn't know whether it was male or female.
        Its parts are so small we couldn't tell."
Dianne laughed. "It's a female.
      You can tell by its white throat.
        The male has a ruby red neck."
"Also we didn't know where to find nectar
      to feed her."
"Hummingbirds eat insects, too," Dianne explained.
      "But we have some nectar from Germany.
        It was just approved by the U. S. Government,
          and the company gave us some free samples."
Dianne brought out a small bottle
      and fed Hummy.
"She has a hollow tongue like a straw
      and sucks up the liquid with it.
        But her pointed bill can also be a fearful weapon.
          Hummingbirds have been seen attacking crows
            when they came too close to their nests."
A week later Hummy was flying about in her cage.
      Her wing was sprained not broken.
She flew straight up, sideways, backwards,
      and could stand or hover in the air
        as she drank from her bottle.

Her wings fluttered so fast
        they were a blur
                and made a soft humming sound.
                        She can fly as fast as a car can travel,
                                fifty or sixty miles an hour.
Hummy was ready to be released
        but winter was coming on.
                Hummingbirds in the wild had departed south
                        where they could find blossoms with nectar.

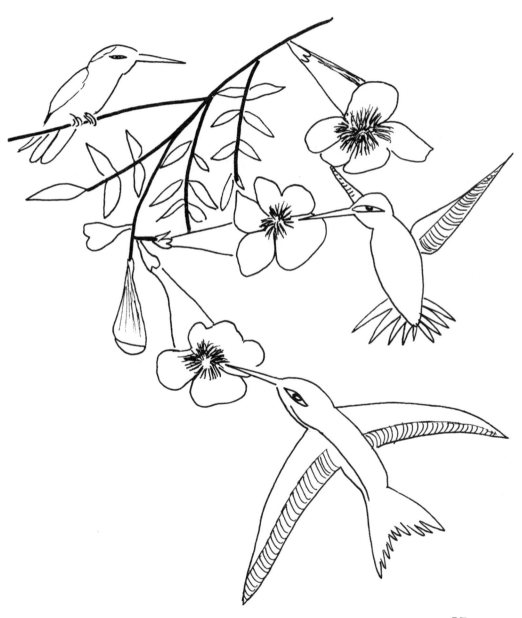

Dianne couldn't let Hummy go
　　　to fly thousands of miles without food.
She could send her south on an airplane
　　　but that would require a special permit,
　　　　　hundreds of dollars for the airplane fare,
　　　　　　　and expenses for a human traveling companion.
The zoo would take her
　　　but Hummy would be kept in captivity
　　　　　for the rest of her life.
This wasn't the fate
　　　Dianne wanted for Hummy.
She decided to convert one of her rooms
　　　into a tropical aviary or home for Hummy.
The aviary was filled with live, green hanging plants
　　　and Hummy wasn't lonesome last winter.
　　　　　Two hummingbirds with damaged wings,
　　　　　　　that were being cared for by another rehabilitator,
　　　　　　　　joined her in her warm quarters.
A zebra finch,
　　　a pet bird,
　　　　　shared the room,
　　　　　　but had to be kept in a cage.
When he flew free,
　　　he attacked Hummy
　　　　　and could have killed her.
In the spring Hummy and one of the hummingbirds
　　　were released into a real garden of sunshine and blossoms.
But sad to tell, the other hummingbird died
　　　during the winter.
The zebra finch is still at the Sanctuary
　　　in a very large cage.
He has calmed down
　　　because he has a mate now to keep him company.

26. Pigeon Heaven

Pigeons, pigeons, pigeons,
    mourning doves, rock doves, ring-necked doves,
      and white show pigeons
        are brought to the Sanctuary
          by ones, twos, threes,
            and the half dozen.
They mate, lay eggs,
    and have more pigeons.
They spread the word around the neighborhood
    about this soup kitchen
      and more pigeons fly into the patio
        for a free handout.

The Sanctuary has become pigeon heaven,
    thought Dianne, when she counted thirty
      eating the corn she had begged from stores
        and was needed by sick and handicapped birds.
She had to do something.
    An idea popped into her mind.
The next weekend she was going to New Jersey,
    two hundred miles away,
      to give a talk at a wildlife refuge.
She would take the well ones with her.
    If she released them far enough away from the Sanctuary,
      they would find other flocks they could join.
Two large cases of mature pigeons
    and two babies were put into the car.
The babies would be left at the refuge,
    a safe place for them to grow up.
It was late at night when Dianne arrived
    at the motel.
The birds couldn't be released in the dark
    because they would be disoriented
      and hopelessly lost.

She covered the cages with blankets.
"Don't you dare open your mouths," she warned them.
Trying to act as though nothing was different or unusual,
she staggered through the lobby to her room
with the heavy cages.
Pets usually aren't allowed in motels
and certainly wild pigeons
wouldn't be welcome.
She stowed the cages in the bathroom
and let the babies flutter around freely.
At dawn the next morning,
she released the adult birds
and hurried inside to clean up the bathroom
which was a mess.
She biked to the refuge,
leaving the baby birds in the bathroom.
She planned to come back for the birds
at lunchtime and clean up the bathroom again.
The morning session was nearly over
when she was called to the telephone.
The motel manager was very angry!
The birds had to go
and so did Dianne!
She was driven back to the motel,
cleaned up the bathroom again,
and took the baby birds to the refuge.
When she got back to the Sanctuary in Maryland the next day,
two of the pigeons she had released in New Jersey
greeted her with open beaks!

27. Pigeon, Pigeon, Who's Got the Pigeon?

The lady who called Dianne
        said there was a pigeon
                in the commuter lane
                        that went around the Pentagon.
The commuter lane is the only one
        where cars are permitted to stop
                to pick up passengers.
The bird couldn't fly, the lady said,
        and was wandering in and out of the traffic
                during the rush hour.
It was endangering its own life
        and could cause accidents
                that might kill or injure people.
The Pentagon,
        the largest building in the world,
                stretches over many acres of land
                        and is across the Potomac River
                                from the Sanctuary.
It has rings
        of superhighways going around or near it,
                a nightmare of mazes for any driver at any time
                        and nearly impossible for a stranger
                                to find his way during rush hour.
It was getting dark when Dianne and her mother
        got into their car
                for the fifty-mile drive to rescue the bird.
Margaret was so intent on her driving
        she didn't see the speed signs.
A policeman pulled them over
        and said they were going thirteen miles
                over the speed limit.

Dianne pleaded with the policeman
    and her story that they were on their way
        to the Pentagon
            to pick up a sick pigeon
                only made him frown.
A likely story,
    he seemed to be thinking.
        Now I've heard them all!
He made them wait
    until he checked
        Margaret's driving record
           on his CB.
When he found out
    that she had no previous tickets or violations,
        he let them go with a warning.
At the Pentagon while Margaret waited
    in the deserted parking lot,
        Dianne walked around and around
           the commuter lane.
In the dark, she crept on her hands and knees under bushes,
    getting scratched and covered with chiggers.
        But no bird was found.
When they got back to the Sanctuary
    at eleven o'clock that night,
        Dianne called the lady
           who had reported the bird.
"Oh," she said. "I called the Animal Control Unit
    after I called you."
Dianne hung up the receiver,
    very carefully,
        controlling her urge to bang it down.
If the Animal Control people
    had picked up the pigeon,
        they would destroy it.

The next day Dianne and her mother
        laughed and laughed.
"What if someone had reported
        seeing me crawling through the bushes
            around the Pentagon
                in the dark of night?" said Dianne.
"Someone who tells tales
        he shouldn't,
            like a stool pigeon," said Margaret.
"The Pentagon could be abuzz today
        with rumors of secret weapons
            and foreign spies!"
                Dianne laughed and laughed
                    as she treated her many chigger bites.

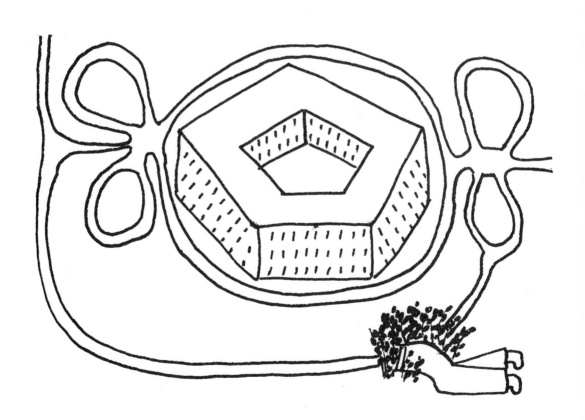

28. The Subway Pigeon

It was very late
　　　on a cold and snowy night
　　　　　when the telephone rang.
Sam Hall,
　　　a fellow conservationist,
　　　　　looked at his clock.
　　　　　　　Midnight, he sighed.
The caller was very excited.
　　　"A sick pigeon is up in the rafters
　　　　　at the Metro Station," said the lady.
"It's been there for days
　　　and must be starving."
Sam drove for miles through the snowstorm
　　　wondering why the lady
　　　　　hadn't called sooner
　　　　　　　or at least before it began to snow.
The station was deserted
　　　because it was so late and
　　　　　the trains had stopped running.
Tired and chilled,
　　　Sam stalked through the empty station
　　　　　with his butterfly net.
An hour went by
　　　and still there was no sight or sound from the bird.
Sam decided to go home
　　　and headed for his car.
　　　　　Suddenly he stopped.
Had he heard a weak coo, coo,
　　　or was it the wind moaning?
He examined the rafters
　　　above his head.
He moved a cardboard box
　　　that someone had placed between the studs.

Wedged behind the box,
        crouched a pigeon.
Sam carefully eased the bird into his net.
        It was covered with thick oil
                and couldn't fly.
Sam also noticed that it had only one leg,
        a possible birth defect.
He took the bird home
        and bathed it every hour with warm mineral oil
                to take off the thick grease.
He had to force-feed it through a tube
        because it was too weak to eat or drink by itself.
When Sam went on vacation,
        he brought the pigeon to the Sanctuary for further care.
It hopped about on the patio
        on its one good leg,
                exercising its wings.
One fine day it flew away,
        its leg tucked under its tail.

29. Oh, Annabell! Oh, Annabell!

The patio at the Sanctuary is always
　　　filled with pigeons
　　　　　but Dianne will never forget
　　　　　　　a white fantail show pigeon,
　　　　　　　　　one of her first birds.
Annabell flew into the Sanctuary
　　　and liked what she saw.
　　　　　She stayed and stayed and stayed.
A few weeks later
　　　Lillybell, a young oriental frill,
　　　　　also a show pigeon,
　　　　　　　was brought to the Sanctuary.
Annabell and Lillybell became good friends,
　　　sharing a nest and their food.
Lillybell grew and matured
　　　and like birds of every feather
　　　　　followed her natural instincts.
　　　　　　　She found mate after mate after mate.
She was an eager, ardent integrationist
　　　and her mates didn't have to be her own kind
　　　　　or an oriental frill.
She chose partners among the rock, ring-necked, mourning doves
　　　and hybrids, birds with mothers and fathers
　　　　　of different breeds,
　　　　　　　that were squatters on the patio.

66

She raised babies by the nestsful.
Workers at the Sanctuary
watched with curiosity
when the babies hatched
trying to guess who the father was.
But Annabell, poor Annabell,
never found a mate.
As Lillybell flitted from bird to bird,
Annabell languished,
became sad, withdrawn,
and refused to eat.
It is said
that she died of a broken heart
while Lillybell carried on and on!

30. Kelly, the Green Heron

Kelly, the green heron,
      stood motionless on the rim of the half-filled bathtub,
            its favorite place in the Sanctuary.
Its long sharp beak
      was pointed toward the ceiling,
            but its unwavering black eyes
                watched every drop of water.
Brown specks were splashed on its long white neck
      and the gray back feathers
            were showing glints of blue green.
"It's an immature bird, and I can't tell its sex," said Dianne.
      "When it is full grown
            and if it is male,
                its neck will be rust colored
                    and its back feathers will be green."
Kelly had been brought to the Sanctuary
      with a broken wing.
            The wing had healed improperly in the wild,
                and Kelly couldn't fly.
The veterinarian,
      who specialized in treating birds,
            told Dianne that he could reset the wing.
He said that birds have hollow bones
      without nerve endings.
The bird shouldn't feel any pain
      except some discomfort from the stretching of the skin
            if he broke the wing again and reset it.
Dianne held the heron so it wouldn't be frightened.
      She felt no movement or reaction in Kelly's body
            as the doctor gently maneuvered the bones
                back in place.

He put a splint on the wing
      and for weeks Kelly
           continued to hop in and out of the bathtub.
When the bandages came off,
      Kelly flew to the shower curtain rod
           where it watched strange creatures
              who invaded its territory.
In the spring
      Kelly was released into a marsh
           where it stands motionless
              pretending it's a blade of grass
                  as it waits for crabs and fish
                     to spear with its sharp beak.

31. Long-Legged Beauties

The game warden thought the great blue heron
    was behaving strangely
        as it wandered on the sandy shore
           at Chesapeake Beach.
It stood with its head held high
    swaying back and forth
        in an aimless way.
A healthy heron would stay in the marshes
    standing motionless for countless minutes
        peering into the shallow water.
Suddenly its head would dart out
    like a striking snake
        to spear a small fish or crab with its beak.
This heron was too young to fly
    and its eyes were blank and staring.
The game warden crept closer and closer,
    and the bird seemed unaware of his presence.
Gently and carefully, the warden
    put his jacket over the bird and picked it up.
He brought it to the Sanctuary,
    and Dianne took it to a veterinarian.
The vet shook his head sadly.
    Both eyes were damaged beyond repair.
But Dianne kept trying to find help.
    She called other veterinarians,
        naturalists, conservationists, and friends.
She located a doctor at Children's Hospital
    who said he would operate on the heron.
        He wasn't sure it would help but he would try.
For many months
    the heron strolled majestically around on the patio
        towering above the squatty ducks and seagulls
           like a graceful ballerina.

Its mature blue-gray feathers grew in
        and when its wings developed,
            Dianne held it firmly,
                letting it exercise by flapping them
                    in imitation of flight.
Small fish and mice were dangled on its beak
        that it would swallow whole.
It would stand quietly without a quiver of fear
        as Dianne stroked its long slender neck.
She planned to make a halter for it
        and take it for walks into the marsh.
It did not live to have the operation.
        It slipped away quietly in its sleep
            from injuries that could not be seen.
But it had lived in comfort and peace
        far beyond the time
            it would have been alive in the wild
                with its sightless eyes.
Recently another heron was brought to the Sanctuary.
        It has a broken knee joint
            and lives in the bathroom
                where Dianne can observe it.
It is very possible
        it can be released
            when the joint is healed.
Dianne has learned,
        that when birds cannot fly
            because of wing damage or other injuries,
                they do not live very long at the Sanctuary.

The beagle was a natural retriever.
    Anything he found,
        old shoes, cans, rags,
           and even live animals,
              he brought to his master.
He would lay these "gifts"
    at his master's feet
        proudly wagging his tail
        and gazing at him
           expecting a pat on the head
           or a kind word.
But the master, who had to return toys to the neighborhood children,
    underwear pulled from a clothesline to an angry housewife,
        and chewed up newspapers to front porches
           wasn't always impressed
           or amused
              by the dog's skill.
His scoldings and disappvoal,
    however, did not stop
        the dog's natural instinct
           to pick up objects.
But the master was shocked one day
    when the dog carefully laid
        what looked like a large hen's egg
        at his feet.
"Did you steal it from a hen house
    or did you find it in the marsh?"
        he shouted at the excited dog.
           "Show me where you found it!"
But the dog only ran around in circles,
    nudging the egg with his nose.

The man looked at the egg
        and then stared at it!
The shell was cracking open!
        He was sure it had been whole
                when the dog had dropped it at his feet.

As he watched
        a beak appeared
                and then the shell shattered,
                        exposing a fuzzy yellow bird.
Was it a chicken, a duck, or a goose?
        Was it a domestic bird or a wild one?
The dog wiggled with delight
        as he sniffed the new arrival.
Certainly this was the best prize
        he had ever brought home,
                he seemed to say with his wildly wagging tail!

But the master was ignoring him.
     He was wrapping
          the tiny creature in a kitchen towel.
He opened a cupboard door
     and grabbed a frying pan,
          the first thing he saw,
              and put the bird in it.
Then he called the Sanctuary.
     "No, you don't," he said to the dog
          when he tried to get into the car
              for the ride to the Sanctuary.
Dianne laughed when she saw the bird in the pan.
     "A duck," she said.
          "But what kind of a duck are you?"
She put it into an incubator
     and fed it.
In a few weeks the fuzzy yellow feathers
     were replaced by bright green ones
          on its head and neck.
Then rusty red plumage appeared on its breast
     and white on its sides.
It was a male mallard,
     one of the most beautiful
          of the wild ducks.

When he was full grown,
     Dianne took him to a pond in a state park
          where he could find a mate.
Dogs can't snatch eggs from nests there
     because dogs aren't allowed in the park!

33. Nestle

The black and brown canvasback duck
    was called Nestle
        because she liked to cuddle
            when Dianne held her.
When her picture was being taken,
    she seemed to be aware of the camera
        and held her head high
            like a fashion model.
She would stare
    with her unseeing eyes
        because she was blind.
Every day Dianne put her into the bathtub
    where she tried to dive in the shallow water.
Canvasback ducks swim underwater
    to the bottom of ponds
        for the wild celery
            they like to eat.
A doctor at Children's Hospital
    said he would operate on her
        and try to restore her sight.
But months after good care and food,
    Dianne found her stiff and cold one morning.
She had quietly died
    from internal injuries
        that had caused her blindness.
But Nestle will never be forgotten.
    There are many pictures in the Sanctuary
        of Dianne and Nestle
            that have appeared
                on the front pages
                    of newspapers and magazines.

34. Quackers and Cheese

Quackers was a down-covered duckling
        when she was found floating in the Bay.
The conservation worker
        who was out in his canoe
                thought she was dead
                        but something told him
                                not to leave her.
                                        He put her in his boat.

A few hours later
        when he came back to the dock,
                he picked up the little bird.
Did he feel a slight heartbeat
        or was it his imagination?
He held her in both hands
        and looked at her carefully.
Yes, not only could he feel
        but he could see the heart throbbing.
                She was alive!

He brought her to the Sanctuary
and Dianne fed and cared for her.
When her mature feathers grew in
she turned into a female mallard
but she had a serious birth defect.
Her wings grew in upside down
called "angel-wings"
and she would never fly.
Dianne often wondered
if the mother was aware of this handicap
and had abandoned her.
Animals that cannot keep up
with their families or flocks
are left to take care of themselves.
Quackers was happy and content at the Sanctuary
and never was alone.
Gabby, another mallard with angel-wings,
lived on the patio, too.
But Quackers' very special friend was Cheese,
a female domestic duck.
They chattered happily to each other.
as they waddled about on the patio
and swam in their kiddies' wading pool.

35. Disco Duck

The duck, a female white Muscovy,
    with a red head
        was peacefully
            picking up seeds in the yard
                when a fox came out of the woods.
He grabbed her by one wing.
    The duck quacked and quacked,
        but the fox hung on.
She ran around and around the yard
    dragging the fox with her.
Suddenly she jumped into the swimming pool
    with the fox clinging to her.
The man of the house
    grabbed a net
        and fished them out.
When he dropped them on the grass,
    the fox scurried back into the woods.
The duck was taken to an animal hospital
    to be destroyed without pain
        because her owner thought
            she couldn't live
                with her injuries.
Cathy, one of the helpers at the hospital,
    examined her
        and couldn't find any internal injuries
        or broken bones.
She put her into the pool to recuperate.
    When she turned to leave,
        the frantic quacking of the bird
            made her turn around.
The duck was sinking!
    Lower and lower she sank
        until only her head
            was above water.

"What kind of a duck are you,
        if you can't swim?" asked Cathy
                as she grabbed the panicky bird from the water.
The bird was so upset
        she had forgotten how to swim!
Cathy brought the duck to the Sanctuary
        and she waddles about on the patio,
                wiggling her fat fanny rhythmically,
                        as she dances to the calls
                                of the crows, seagulls, and geese.
"Well, if you can't swim,
        you can dance," said Cathy
                and named her Disco Duck.

36. Cheese Did It!

The telephone caller said
    that a domestic duck
        was swimming about in a pond in Bowie
           and was in danger of losing its life.
Someone may have left it there
    or it could have wandered away from a farm.
It was starving
    because it couldn't find its own food.
But the neighborhood boys were a worse threat.
    They were teasing it, chasing it,
        and using it for target practice
          with their BB guns.
Neighbors had called the Society for the Prevention of Cruelty to Animals
    and the Animal Control Center.
These organizations sent out workers
    who had been trying to catch the duck with nets.
But it always disappeared
    when they came within sight of the bird!

But Dianne knew what to do!
It was spring
and mating season
was in full swing!
She took Cheese,
her female domestic duck, to the pond.
Putting a halter on Cheese,
she walked her to the bank
where the disappearing duck
was frequently seen.
Within five seconds,
out popped the male duck
in pursuit of Cheese.
He followed them to Dianne's car
and hopped in after Cheese.
The love affair continued at the Sanctuary
and there may be ducklings waddling about on the patio
next spring.

37. Ducks Don't Drink Beer

There couldn't be two people mean enough
    to put a plastic six-pack beer holder
        around the neck of a duck,
            but Dianne wasn't sure.
The Sanctuary received two reports,
    at different times and at different places,
        about ducks in this predicament.
Dianne went to the pond in Greenbelt
    where the first report came from
        and paddled around in a kayak for an hour
            but couldn't find the duck.
It was a week later that an animal control officer called
    and said that he had seen a male mallard, perhaps the same one,
        with a plastic beer can holder wrapped around his head
        at Lake Waterford Park,
            about fifteen miles from Greenbelt.
The officer reported that the day before
    volunteer firemen at Powhattan Beach Station
        had been searching for the duck for hours
        in their rescue boat.
When they spotted it,
    the panicky duck took off into the woods.
The water was too shallow
    for the boat to get close to the shore
        and one of the firemen dressed in his bulky uniform
        jumped into the forty-degree water
            to try to catch the duck.
But the mallard got away from him
    in the thick underbrush.
Dianne offered to help them catch the elusive duck
    and the next day
        she and two volunteers met the firemen at their dock.
Armed with long-handled hoop nets
    they began their search of the lake in the rescue boat.

After cruising about for hours,
    they spotted the injured animal
        and tried to creep up on it.
Again the frightened bird took off into the woods.
    Two firemen jumped out of the boat in pursuit
        and managed to capture it in a net.
Dianne cut off the offending plastic
    and was about to release it
        but noticed that its tongue was cut and bleeding.
She brought the duck back to the Sanctuary
    and cared for it until it could eat on its own
        before she released it.
And if the duck could talk,
    it would surely tell us
        that plastic beer can holders
            belong in the trash
                and shouldn't decorate ducks.

38. Now You See Them, Now You Don't

With their long crest feathers
    that hang down their necks,
        male wood ducks look as if they're wearing helmets.
But unlike soldiers,
    who are supposedly aggressive,
        wood ducks are shy creatures.
They are so elusive
    that they are seldom seen in the wild.
        From reports received at the Sanctuary,
            five of them kept appearing and disappearing
                from the streets of Georgetown.

The first caller said he had seen
        five of them waddling about in a parking lot.
When John Vincent returned the call,
        the man said they were gone.
Later that day a worker at the D.C. Animal Control Center
        left a message on the telephone machine
            that they had a female wood duck and a seagull.
A few months ago the workers would have destroyed these animals,
        but now they always check with Dianne
            to see if she will provide foster care
                for any of their strays.
When Dianne picked up the birds,
        she noticed that the wings of the wood duck were clipped
            and there was a tag on one wing of the duck.
The next day there was a call
        from Georgetown Hospital.
            Someone had captured a male wood duck.
When John picked it up,
        he was told there was another duck
            wandering about downstairs in the boiler room.

If he wanted it,
        he would have to catch it.
When he looked at the huge room,
        two stories high and covering a city block,
            he knew why they hadn't caught it.
For two hours he chased the frightened bird
        as it fluttered in and out and around the pipes.
Seven people from the Hospital staff
        joined him in the game of hide and seek.
The frantic bird hopped up on the pipes,
        just out of reach,
            scooted in and out of boxes,
                and flew around the boilers,
                    and then disappeared for long minutes.
John and his helpers looked in and around the machinery
        and up on the pipes.
            They opened the door to a small generator.

There he was
        crouched on it
                without a way of escape.
These two male birds also had their wings clipped
        and tags were fastened on them.
They weren't U. S. Government bands
        which are put on the leg of a bird.
Dianne thought they may have been part of some experiment
        and advertised for the owners
                but no one called for them.
She will keep them at the Sanctuary until spring
        when their feathers grow back in
                and they can fly free.
But she often wonders
        what happened to the other two ducks.
She hopes they found their way
        to freedom in the Potomac River
                which is not far from the streets of Georgetown.

39. To the Rescue!

Eleven-year-old Dana
    called the Sanctuary
        and said that fifteen of their ducks,
            mallards and domestic,
                were in trouble.
Diesel oil had seeped into their pond in Bowie,
    and the ducks were covered with it.
Dianne knew exactly what to do
    and that she had to do it fast.
The year before she had organized
    a workshop for this type of emergency
        and had recruited thirty volunteers
            to take a course
                on how to save animals
                    caught in an oil spill.
Because of her knowledge and work,
    the Sanctuary had been named
        an official emergency care unit
            by the state of Maryland.
A friend of Dana's family had called the state agency
    and that's how Dana knew about Dianne and her work.
Dianne told Dana she would come for the ducks
    if she could catch them.
Dana and her sister, Susan,
    asked their friends to help them,
        and eight teenagers came to the rescue.
Floundering about in an old rowboat
    in the mud and freezing water,
        they caught and recaught the slick birds
            that kept slipping out of their arms.
They rounded up ten of the ducks
    before it became too dark to continue their search.

Dianne and John picked up the birds in Bowie
        and it was ten o'clock that night
                when they got back to the Sanctuary.
The first thing they had to do
        was to keep the birds warm.
Unlike crude oil which only coats the feathers,
        the diesel oil had penetrated the feathers
                so they couldn't be fluffed up
                        and trap air to keep the ducks warm.
Using blankets, boxes, a child's Brite Lite,
        a bed cradle with heat lamps, and a hair dryer,
                John rigged up two makeshift incubators.
Then they began to bathe the ducks
        in a warm, gentle detergent
                but the oil was so thick
                        it didn't soak off.
They had to scrape it off
        with their hands.
Furthermore, the odor of the oil
        made Dianne and John so nauseous
                they couldn't eat for days.

Dianne noticed that the ducks also weren't eating
        but more important
                they weren't drinking
                        and could become dehydrated.
She had to force them to drink
        but needed a special solution of salt and sugar
                such as hospitals use
                        for people on intravenous feedings.
She called the Southern Maryland Hospital at midnight
        and a policeman friend picked up
                twelve bottles of the serum
                        that he delivered
                                to the Sanctuary
                                        before dawn.
Dianne and John worked all through the night—
        washing, force-watering them through a tube,

and supervising the incubators
       so the ducks didn't become too hot or too cold.
The next day Dana's family
     brought in four more ducks,
        and Dianne and John went through the same process again.
Dana's family wondered
     what had happened to the fifteenth duck.
        They searched and searched for it
           but it couldn't be found.
For three days and nights,
     Dianne and John continued
        bathing, feeding, and caring for the ducks
          with hardly a bite to eat.
Ten of the fourteen ducks survived
     and were taken back to their pond in Bowie
        when it was cleaned up.
The story appeared in five newspapers
     and it is hoped that more people will become
        as dedicated to saving our wildlife
          as the workers at the Sanctuary.

40. Epilogue to the Rescue

About two months later
      a man called the Sanctuary
            about a male mallard.
The duck couldn't float!
      He had found the duck
            wandering around in Bowie
                  and had been taking care of him.
Very strange, thought Dianne,
      and asked him to bring the duck
            to the Sanctuary.
When she opened the box,
      she knew she had the fifteenth bird
            that had disappeared
                  from Dana's pond.
The odor of the diesel oil
      was so strong
            it made Dianne gag.
The thick grease was still on his feathers
      and that's why he couldn't float.
She bathed Ed,
      as she began to call him,
            and had to treat him
                  for skin burns.
A few weeks later,
      Ed was floating and swimming
            in the kiddies' wading pool.
He is free to take off
      and find the pond in Bowie
            but keeps hanging around the Sanctuary.
                  He knows where he can get good care!

41. Squirrels of Every Color

Dianne has a license
    to treat small mammals
        as well as birds.
Her most numerous and frequent patients
    are squirrels.
One winter she had fifty cages of squirrels
    in her garage.
They had been born late in the fall
    and had been separated from their mothers.
        They couldn't be released in the cold winter
           when food is scarce.
Dianne fed them all winter
    and released them in the spring.
But two other squirrels she had nursed for weeks
    and that had required special care and treatment
        would not be forgotten at the Sanctuary.

Construction workers cut down a tree
　　and didn't know
　　　　a nest of squirrels was in it.
The frightened mother scampered off.
　　　　When the babies were brought to the Sanctuary,
　　　　　　they were about five or six weeks old.
Only one of the squirrels survived the fall,
　　　　but Sneezy, as Dianne named him, was very sick.
Dianne kept Sneezy beside her bed
　　　　and set her alarm to awaken her
　　　　　　because she had to feed him every hour.
Mammals have to be fed day and night
　　　　unlike birds that will sleep throughout the dark hours
　　　　　　if they are not disturbed.
Dianne made a special formula for Sneezy
　　　　and squeezed the food into his mouth
　　　　　　from a sterilized eyedropper.
She rubbed his nose with Vicks,
　　　　cleared his throat with a baby aspirator, and
　　　　　　medicated him with baby aspirin.
She even took him in a shoe box to meetings with her
　　　　so he wouldn't miss a feeding.
Sneezy grew up
　　　　to be a healthy, full-grown squirrel
　　　　　　and one day scampered over the fence
　　　　　　　　to live in the trees around the Sanctuary.

But Wapanik was a squirrel of a different color.
　　　　The Humane Society volunteer received a call
　　　　　　from a lady about a squirrel
　　　　　　　　that had fallen out of its nest.
The mother had not picked it up
　　　　nor taken it back into the tree.
Strange behavior for a mother
　　　　but perhaps she wasn't sure
　　　　　　this creature belonged to her.

It was different
        with its bright red eyes
                and its white, not gray, fur.
An albino, the volunteer explained,
        without pigmentation or melanin,
                a part of the body
                        that gives skin and hair their colors.
He suggested it be taken
        to the Sanctuary.
Although it was dragging its feet,
        Dianne could find no broken bones
                when she examined it,
                        but it was dazed by the fall.
A volunteer called the Smithsonian Institution
        and was told that the Delaware Indian name
                for a white squirrel was "wapanik."
After a few days of rest,
        Wapanik was taken to Bobbi Sweeney,
                a wildlife rehabilitator
                        who takes care of small mammals.
Bobbi had twenty-six squirrels at the time
        and put Wapanik in a cage with a melanistic squirrel.
This one was black not gray
        because it had more melanin
                than the usual squirrel.
Human beings also have melanin.
        The color of your skin
                depends upon the amount of melanin in your body.
Wapanik will remain at this Refuge
        for the rest of its life.
Albino squirrels are weaker
        than their colored brothers and sisters.
Also because of their whiteness
        or lack of color,
                they are easy to see
                        and would be caught by owls and hawks,
                                their enemies.

42. The Little Thieves or Ferrets

The calls come and come to the Sanctuary,
    calls about birds and animals,
        strange and unusual.
The man on the telephone said that he was working
    in an empty apartment house
        and had seen an unknown animal
            scampering around in the rooms.
It was white, gray, and black
    about the size of a cat
        but longer and sleeker
           with a furry tail.
"If it looks like a mink or weasel," said Dianne,
    "it could be a ferret!"
If he could catch it,
    she would be glad to give it a home.

Dianne's license also includes permission
            to care for small mammals.
She told the man
            that this animal could have been someone's pet,
                        and the owners may have abandoned it.
Ferrets have a musky odor
            that some people do not like.
Although they are sold in pet stores,
            she would not recommend them as pets
                        for children.
They have very sharp teeth
            and will bite if they are abused or mishandled.
Once upon a time
            they were used to hunt mice and rats
                        from burrows or underground homes.
They originally came from Africa
            and need a warm climate to survive.
The man brought the slinky animal
            to the Sanctuary in a paper bag.
Dianne stroked the silky fur
            before she put it into a cage with food.
The next day the man appeared again
            with another paper bag.
                        The ferret had a mate!
They will keep the Sanctuary free of mice and rats
            and children will be able to see them
                        dig tunnels in the ground.
Ferret means "little thief" in Latin
            but so far they've only stolen the affection
                        of the volunteers at the Sanctuary.

43. The Three-Legged Fox

Mike, a sixteen year old,
    had called many wildlife agencies
        without success
            before he dialed the Sanctuary.
He wanted someone to help him release a fox
    caught in a vicious steel trap.
Even though it was a cold and rainy night,
    John Vincent couldn't resist
        Mike's pleas for help.
They walked a mile down a dark and muddy trail,
    carrying a small cage.
John hoped this wasn't a joke or snipe hunt.
    Some kids might think it was funny
        to lead an adult on a hunt
        for a snipe
            that doesn't exist.
Also, the hunter who had set the trap
    could have come for the animal
        or might be on his way to check on his trap.
John didn't want to meet an angry trapper
    out here in the dark!
After trudging through the rain and mud
    for half an hour,
        they found the snarling fox
            with one of his hind feet caught in the trap.
John put on his heavy gloves
    and hung a snare or noose
        around the neck of the frantic animal.
He held the head
    with its sharp teeth
        away from them
            as Mike released the trap.

They carefully guided him
    into the cage
        and tramped back to the car.
The next morning Dianne took the fox
    to the veterinarian,
      and he said
        the leg was broken in three places.
He put a splint on it
    but during the night
      the confused animal chewed it off
        and the vet had to amputate the leg.
After a few weeks,
    the fox was still snarling at visitors
      but moving about in his cage
        with ease and speed.
John released him at Cedarville State Park
    where there are acres and acres of woodland
      and no traps.
The fox hopped out of the cage,
    tested his three legs,
      and looked around at John,
        as though saying thank-you
          before running into the woods.

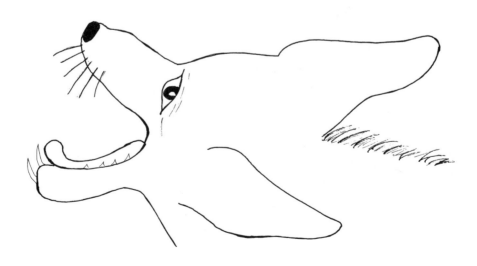

But Dianne's and John's work is not over.
The following Sunday they attended
a rally on the Washington Monument grounds
with thousands
of other wildlife conservationists.
They are trying to persuade congressmen
to pass laws
to make these traps illegal.
These traps have been used
since the days of slavery when they were used
to catch slaves
who tried to run away.
Now they are supposedly used only
for trapping wild animals
but dogs and other pets get caught in them.
Animals can't protest,
not in words,
and people must speak for them.

44. A Trio of Fawns

The Maryland Department of Natural Resources
    asked Dianne to raise a fawn, a baby deer,
        until it could feed itself.
The deer would then be given
    a home at the Baltimore zoo.
If the fawn had been a male,
    he would have been destroyed
        if his mother could not be found.
People at the Department of Natural Resources
    had made this rule.
The scientists said
    that male deer are too hard to raise in captivity
        and when grown up
            become mean and nasty.
A child had recently
    been attacked
        and injured by a buck.
Dianne was very upset by this rule
    and called the governor's office
        to suggest the rule be changed.
Only a very few deer
    would lose their mothers,
        and she offered to take the orphans.
While she was talking to a secretary
    in the governor's office,
        two women brought in another female fawn.
They said they had found her in a field
    and couldn't find the mother.
They took her in their home,
    played with her,
        and fed her grass and cereal.
They had brought her to the Sanctuary
    because she was very sick,
        and they didn't know what to do for her.

Dianne said that fawns
        should have a special diet
                and not people food.
She also told the women
        that mother deer leave their babies
                during the daytime
                        and will come back at night
                                to feed them.
But this fawn was too sick
        to be taken back to her mother
                even if she could be found.
She needed twenty-four-hour care.
        Dianne called the vet,
                and a volunteer came
                        to give the fawn an injection.
Wild animals also become ill
        and die from stress
                or being handled by people.

In the midst of her twenty-four-hour program
of intensive care for the fawns,
Dianne heard about a woman
on a farm in Virginia
who was raising fawns.
This woman also raised goats
and had discovered that the mother goats or nannies
would become foster mothers for the fawns.
Nanny goats will nurse baby deer,
but they need to be introduced to the idea
very carefully and gently
in order
to accept these strange orphans.
The two fawns did not live,
but a few days later
another male deer was brought to the Sanctuary.
Dianne called the farmer in Virginia
who said she would take the deer
if Dianne brought it to her.
It was very late on Friday afternoon
when Dianne called the office
in Richmond, Virginia,
to get permission
to take the animal into the state.

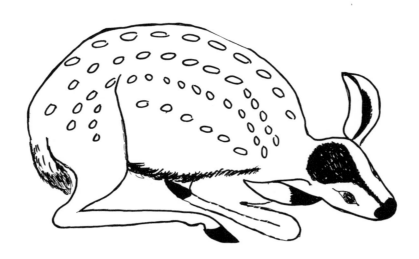

She was told she needed a certificate indicating
    that the deer was in good health.
She took the fawn to the vet,
    and he signed the health certificate.
Dianne and John drove for two hours
    to a Potomac River bridge
        to meet the naturalist from Richmond.
He had also driven
    for hours to meet them.
They exchanged the health certificate
    for the permission slip
        and drove for hundreds of miles
            to deliver the fawn
                to the woman with the goats.
Dianne has had reports from the farm
    that the fawn is healthy
        and has been adopted by a nanny goat.
The Maryland Department of Natural Resources
    now sends any orphan fawns, male or female,
    to the Sanctuary
        for their expert care.
And most important of all,
    the fawns will not be killed
        if they lose their mothers.

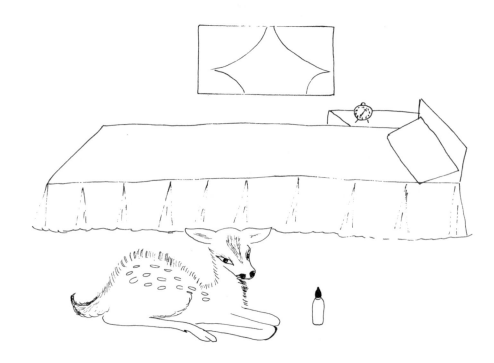

45. A Deer Not So Dear!

It was a Saturday night
>when a policeman from another county called
>>about a deer that had been hit
>>>by a car.

He thought the doe
>could be saved
>>but needed care
>>>until she became conscious.

Dianne called Cathy Wilcox
>and with John and Margaret
>>they drove to the other county
>>>in Cathy's pickup truck.

The policeman had the deer in the trunk of his cruiser.
>He had handcuffed her feet together
>>so she couldn't kick or thrash about
>>>when she became conscious.

John tied up her feet
>before the policeman took off the handcuffs.

He helped them carry the deer
>to Cathy's truck.
>>Margaret carefully tucked a blanket around the animal
>>>and began to laugh and laugh.

The blanket she had grabbed,
>when she left the Sanctuary,
>>was a wedding gift
>>>from her parents
>>>>forty years ago.

They took the deer
>to the Emergency Animal Clinic,
>>and the vet examined it.

The animal didn't have any broken bones
>but there were a few cuts and bruises
>>on her legs.

When they arrived at the Sanctuary,
      Dianne called Gary Boag in California,
            who specializes in caring for deer,
                for his advice.
He warned that deer are very dangerous
      when frightened or hurt
            and to be extra cautious
                when she became conscious.
The four of them
      carried her into the basement
            and she came to for a few minutes.
They quickly put her down
      and moved away from her legs.
            Even with her feet tied,
                she kicked a hole in the storm door.
After they got her into the basement,
      she came to
            and kicked a hole in the wall.
They had to get her out of there
      before she knocked down the wall
            and injured herself.

Dianne called a friend in Upper Marlboro
    and he said Dianne could put the deer
        in his tobacco barn.
However, it had many loose boards in it
    that would have to be nailed down.
John went to take care of the barn
    and Cathy called Gary in California again.
She wanted to know what kind of sedative,
    and the amount to use
        so they could take the deer to the barn.
He suggested Rompum
    and warned that the dosage
        would only last for a half-hour.
While Dianne and Margaret tried to distract the frantic animal,
    Cathy dashed in
        and gave it
        a shot in the rump.
As soon as the doe was out,
    Dianne tended to her wounds.
        Then Dianne, Cathy, and Margaret
        tugged, pulled, and carried her back into the truck.
As they drove to the barn,
    they hoped and prayed
        she wouldn't come to
        and kick a hole in the truck.
Also, how would they untie her legs
    if she were kicking?
Luckily, the deer was still unconscious
    when they carried her into the barn
        and cut the ropes.
They stayed in the truck all night,
    checking on the deer
        through the cracks in the boards.
She came to later than they thought she would
    and began running around in the barn,
        kicking at the boards
        trying to get out.

Dianne was relieved to see her
    that active
        because it meant she had no internal injuries.
The next morning Dianne called the game warden.
    He peeked in at her,
        and told them they could release her.
When John opened the door,
    Dianne and Cathy were well out of the way,
        around the corner of the barn.
The doe shot out of the barn so fast
    they didn't even see
        her white tail disappearing in the woods
            before they came around the other side of the barn!

46. The Groundhog or Woodchuck

A mother and her small son
    brought the woodchuck
        to the Sanctuary.
It was very sick
    and only a few weeks old.
John, who was on duty at the time,
    questioned the mother and little boy.
They said they had found it in a field
    on the Eastern Shore.
After much questioning John learned
    they had seen the mother
        but the father had been shot by the farmer.
The parents had picked up the baby groundhog or woodchuck
    because they wanted their son
        to have the experience of raising a wild animal.
They had known a child
    who had had a wild animal for a pet.
John gritted his teeth
    and explained why a child
        should not raise a wild animal.
Even experienced rehabilitators,
    such as Dianne,
        with all their knowledge
            lose many babies.

Wild animal babies need very special diets,
    each one requiring
        what their parents
            would feed them in the wild.
Furthermore, these animals also die from stress.
    You can cause stress in animals
        by handling them too much.

Babies grow up to be animals
        that must be able to protect themselves.
This means they grow sharp teeth and claws
        in order to survive in the wild.
People are also enemies
        that threaten their survival.
Wild animals might even attack the person
        who was their adopted parent.
If you want to release a wild animal into the wild,
        you must train it to defend itself,
                catch its own prey,
                        and find its own food.

After John explained all this to the mother,
        she again asked her son if he wanted
                to leave the woodchuck at the Sanctuary!
John did not grit his teeth this time!
        Firmly and as a policeman,
                which he is, he told them
                        that the child could not have the animal.
It was against the law
        for people to have wild animals and birds
                without a permit.
He made it quite clear
        that the animal must stay at the Sanctuary
                because Dianne had such a permit and could
                        care for this woodchuck!
John worked on the sick animal
        for hours,
                massaging it to get it breathing regularly,
                        warming it,
                                and feeding it a special formula
                                        that wouldn't
                                                make it sicker.

A few months later
    the groundhog was healthy
        but also snarling
            and showing its sharp teeth,
                even to John who had saved its life!
But that's the way
    a wild animal must be,
        if they were to release it into the woods!

47. Cats, Cats, Cats!

Dianne does not want the Sanctuary
    overrun with neglected pets.
There are other shelters for them,
    and she needs her food
        for her wildlife.
But cats seem to find her.
    New Kitty, a long-haired gray-striped kitten,
        walked into the Antique Shop.
She was declawed
    and couldn't protect herself.
        Nor did she have a collar.
Dianne advertised for her owners
    but no one claimed her.
Missy, who turned into Mystery,
    came from the pound.
Dianne was told the cat was a female
    but was actually a male
        and that's why he was called Mystery.
           No one knew his sex.
There is also Caspar,
    a big, tan and white Tom,
        and Pumpkin, white with orange patches.
Pumpkin had sprawled legs
    that stuck out of his sides
        like a turtle's feet.
He lacked a certain vitamin in his body,
    and when it was included in his diet
        his legs straightened out.
People ask if the big, tiger-striped one
    with the black rings on its tail
        is a Maine coon cat.

The newest and youngest has a mask
    on its face,
        and is called Bandit.
Bandit was found in the machine shop
    at the Pentagon.
The men were teasing it
    and said they were going to put
        it in the dishwasher!
Art Growden, a Sanctuary volunteer,
    snatched up the kitten,
        took the rest of the day off from his job,
          and drove fifty miles
            to the Sanctuary with it.
All six cats sniff at visitors,
    climb in their laps,
        peer at the baby squirrels in the incubator,
          but no bird has been lost to them.
Maybe they know their haven
    is also a retreat for other animals.
But it could be
    that they are too well fed
        and too lazy to catch a bird.

48. Corky, the Cockatiel

A radio announcer
    at a station in the city
        called the Sanctuary
            and said they had a small parrot or cockatiel.
"It's someone's pet.
    We've advertised for the owner
        but no one has called us.
            Will you take the bird?"
When Dianne arrived at the office,
    he explained that the bird had been sitting
        on the eighth-floor window ledge
            and had been trying to get into the window.
But that was the problem.
    The windows in the building were sealed.
They couldn't reach the bird from the ground
    or from the twelfth-floor roof.
Someone had the bright idea
    of lowering a perch from the roof.
        The cockatiel might hop onto it.
It was quite a feat, he continued,
    to let down a perch on a rope
        from that height.
The perch swayed in the wind
    and they carefully moved it
        to swing in front of, but not to hit,
            the cockatiel.
If it hit the cockatiel,
    the frightened bird might take off again!
It was many, many long minutes
    before the bird hopped onto the perch.
No one dared cheer
    until the little parrot
        was safely in the hands of one of the rescuers.

"Quite a story!" said Dianne
        as she put the bird in her cage.
                "It's a beauty!"
Its light gray feathers,
        highlighted by its white wings and breast,
                glistened in the sunlight.
But its most striking features
        were its yellow-gold head
                and a circle of pink on each cheek
                        so perfect it looked as though
                                it had been painted.
Dianne also advertised for the owners,
        but no one called her.
Corky can say, "Pretty bird!"
        and "What are you doing?"
A few weeks ago
        you could hear its piercing wolf whistles
                when you came into the Sanctuary.
But Corky isn't whistling at people
        any longer!
He has a cagemate now,
        a female cockatiel,
                and gives her all his attention.
"Corky and his mate
        will be very special birds
                to show children and parents," said Dianne.
"This is the type of pet
        they should have
                and not try to tame a wild one."

49. How to Be a Bird Nurse

You can become a bird caretaker
        but you must have a license
                or written permission
                        from a state or the federal government
                                to care for injured wild birds
                                        and small mammals.
You must study,
        take courses, read books,
                and prove to two licensed caretakers
                        that you know what to do
                                and how to care for injured birds.
You must have big and little cages,
        a fenced yard,
                and a special room for recuperating birds.
If you have a pond
        or are near some water,
                you may take care of water birds.
If you want to rehabilitate raptors,
        birds of prey,
                such as owls and hawks,
                        you must have large flight cages
                                for them to practice flying
                                        and catch live prey.
Only in emergencies
        may eagles be taken
                by licensed rehabilitators.
If you find an injured eagle,
        call a park ranger
                who will take it to a special refuge
                        for these endangered birds.

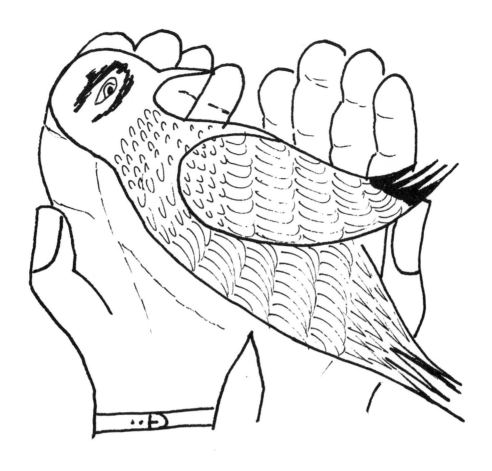

Domestic animals and pets,
      dogs, cats, canaries, rabbits,
           cows, horses, chickens,
                are cared for by veterinarians.
But Dianne has found a few animal doctors
      who will examine, operate, and prescribe medication
           for her wild animal patients,
                if she doesn't know what to do for them.
Rehabilitators work without pay!
      They may not charge for their services
           but can accept donations
                to help pay for food and medicines.

50. A New Home for Birds and Beasts

The telephone rings and rings,
    day and night,
        asking for help
          and more help
            for animals in distress.
But this call was different!
    A gift!
        A gift of fifty-two acres of woodland in Brandywine.
Dianne looked about her house,
    a house that was no longer a home for people.
Her living room was stuffed with typewriters,
    a Xerox machine, file cabinets, desks, and
        cages for Corky and the ferrets.
Sprawled over the posters and newsletters
    were six cats.
One of the bedrooms had been converted
    into an aviary for hummingbirds and a zebra finch.
The green heron and Nestle, the diving duck,
    had lived in the bathroom.
The recreation room and garage were piled to the ceiling
    with bags of birdseed,
        cages for squirrels,
          the three-legged fox,
            and neglected parakeets from
              a former pet store.
Six incubators
    and a variety of items
        for the Thrift Shop
          were tucked in corners.
The demanding chirping of the fifty-odd baby birds
    was deafening when you opened the door
        to the utility room.

And in Dianne's bedroom lay a week-old baby fawn
        that she was giving twenty-four-hour intensive care.
Out on the patio were more cages with a baby woodchuck;
          crows that once were pets and couldn't be rehabilitated;
              rabbits, ducks, and chickens, Easter pets
                  that had been discarded
                      when they were no longer cute and fuzzy.
Crowded into the small fenced-in patio
        was the usual menagerie
          of geese, ducks, seagulls, and pigeons.
Two large flight cages,
        for Mariah, the golden eagle,
          and nine owls,
              guarded by two beagles,
                  were outside the stockade fence.
Animals of all kinds,
        from peacocks to pigeons,
          fawns to ferrets,
              big, little, beautiful, mean, ugly, and vicious
                find shelter at the Sanctuary.
They live in comfort and peace,
        or fly away to freedom
          after being restored to health.
These natural resources are being protected
        because Dianne, Margaret, John Vincent, and the many volunteers
          not only give of their time, money, and talents
              but have a profound reverence for life
                in the humblest of God's creatures.
The animals seem to sense this caring
        and respond by getting well.
In 1983 the Sanctuary cared for 261 animals
        and of those 184 survived
          or about 70%.
Most conservationists report
        about a 50% survival rate.
At the end of August 1984
        the Sanctuary had cared for 600 animals.

This house is about to explode,
thought Dianne.
But it would be months, perhaps years,
before the new land
could be a home
for her and her charges.
In the meantime she had leased
a farm in Bowie.
It had acres of land for large flight cages;
room for a pond for the water birds;
protected woodland away from hunters
and careless children with BB guns.
It would be a safe haven for crippled mothers to raise babies;
a laboratory for naturalists;
and a school where children can learn about wildlife.
A vision of what can be,
she thought as she stroked the fawn,
but much work, money, time, and volunteers
will be needed
before the dream comes true.